EVEN THE BIRDS WILL PAY

God's Ultimate Plan of Restoration

SAYO AKINTOLA

COVENANT PUBLISHING

Even the Birds Will Pay: God's Ultimate Plan of Restoration
Sayo Akintola

Unless otherwise stated, all scripture quotations are taken from the Holy Bible, King James Version (KJV). Other versions cited are NIV, NKJV, NASB, TS98, TJB and WEB.

ISBN 978-1-907734-22-9

First Edition, First Printing August 2017

Covenant Publishing
samadewunmi@btinternet.com

Covenant Publishing is part of New Covenant Church
Charity Registered in England & Wales number 1004343
Registered Address: 506-510 Old Kent Road. LONDON SE1 5BA

Cover Design by Covenant Publishing Team
Published by Covenant Publishing
Printed in the United Kingdom

TABLE OF CONTENT

Dedication

To all of my Fathers in faith who had taught me that legacy is more precious than currency.

- Pastor Omololu Adegoke
  The Lord Reigns Ministries, Ibadan
- Evangelist Mathew Owojaiye
  Food For The Total Man, Kaduna
- Revd. Emmanuel Olasupo Ajao
  Associate General Overseer, New Covenant Church Worldwide
- Rev. Dr Paul Jinadu
  General Overseer, New Covenant Church Worldwide
- The other main influences in my walk with the Lord.

Acknowledgement

To God alone be all the glory because what seems impossible is made possible without sweat because of grace.

With some people, the ability to write is a gift. You need to know my story. I started a MSc in Public Administration programme at Obafemi Awolowo University, Ile-Ife, in Nigeria. I did so well in all of my academic courses, but the only thing that remained to be awarded the degree was to turn in my thesis. Unfortunately, I got stuck and till today the Master of Science in Public Administration is still a mirage. So, to write 'Stones', my first book, and this second book is nothing but GRACE. So I celebrate God for this massive grace.

My wife and the mother of my children; thank you – my friend and partner in ministry. Thank you for believing in me. Your faith in me and our ministry makes me walk more carefully. May you continue to soar high in God and ministry.

My two wonderful children Marvellous and David; you are part of my message, and I am learning from you by the day.

Bro. Paul and Mummy Kate; you are gems of inestimable value. The story of our lives will not be complete without your contributions.

Rev. Emmanuel Ajao, my father, my friend and my mentor, you are great sir.

My Deputy General Overseer, Revd. Obafemi Omisade; thank you sir, you a man with a big heart.

New Covenant Church Woolwich; you are my home, and I appreciate this family of God.

Revd. Ayo Olufemi Jotham; thank you for your efforts to read and work on the raw materials.

Kemi Emmanuel and Sola Sonuga; I say big thank you for proofing and editing my book. Lekan and Toyin Labode; you are a great source of encouragement.

Pastor Yinka Sonuga; your contributions are much appreciated.

Pastor Sam Adewunmi my brother and publisher; I am so grateful.

All the pastors around the world, it's such a privilege to serve God together in His vineyard.

The purpose of this book is not to show my academic or intellectual prowess but so that I can help someone in one way or another.

Thank you so very much.

Sayo Akintola

Foreword

This book gives insight into the difficult issues that people go through in life and their root causes. It also reveals the grace of God to overcome such difficulties and trials. There is no situation, or problem, no matter how far gone, that God cannot resolve, and He will also alongside, grant full restoration where required.

I believe those who have unresolved issues in their lives and read this book will be encouraged to know that with God, there is always a way out, and they will glean the necessary steps to obtain victory.

The author is a seasoned minister that has enjoyed the faithfulness of God in his life, home and ministry.

This book, therefore, comes highly recommended.

Obafemi Omisade
Deputy General Overseer,
New Covenant Church, UK

EVEN THE BIRDS WIL PAY

Even the Birds will Pay

There will be no way we can talk about restoration without the mention of a great woman in 2 Kings 4.

This woman provided free accommodation and comfort to Elisha without any strings attached. I was amazed to note that despite her heartache and need, she was ready to meet the need of a prophet. God had not blessed her with the fruit of the womb.

It's also of note that she never at any time discussed the challenge with the man of God who resided in her house until the man of God began to ask questions on how to repay her for such kindness. Gehazi, Elisha's assistant then told the man of God of the barrenness of this family.

Here also, the reluctance of this great woman not to bother Elisha on the issue of her barrenness was not going to deter the man of God from prophesying the blessing of a son to this family. According to the working of the God of Elisha, the woman gave birth to a boy just as it was prophesied. God honoured the word of His servant and brought great joy to this woman. Not long after, the young boy died, and everything looked bleak and uncertain. Instead of this woman to despair or become worried, she went quietly to the man of God. She concluded that if a man can prophesy something that was not meant to become a reality, then this man can also speak recovery to a dead situation. So she refused to bury the dead boy and went instead to the man of God. She knew the God of restoration in a very personal way.

On getting to the man of God, she calmly reported the situation. Even though the man of God was unaware of the development as he had not been pre-warned or instructed by God, he did not break down or glorify the devil. He knew that there is nothing impossible for our great God to do. He was not even going to rush out to solve the problem; so he sent Gehazi with his rod, with specific instructions on how to handle the situation.

With Gehazi, something must have gone wrong before he arrived at the house where this boy was laid and when he placed the staff of the Prophet on the kid, nothing happened. Elisha then decided to visit the scene by himself. When he saw the boy's still body, he was unaffected by the impossibilities and the negatives. He just laid on the corpse and did a transference of life from himself to this boy, just like when one is trying to charge a dead battery with an active battery. That was the end of the woman's agony.

So restoration is capable of reversing death. Many scriptural references put paid to the fact that God can reverse even the coldest circumstances of death. Lazarus came back to life after four days in the grave. Dorcas was restored back to life. What about Jairus' daughter? It your season of restoration. Anything dead is coming back to life; even things that are about to die receive restoration in Jesus name.

One of the great lessons to learn from this wonderful woman of faith is in 2 Kings 8:1-12.

This same woman who in 2 Kings 4 provided accommodation and succour to the man of God, did not realise that her act of kindness was a seed she was sowing into her future. Her generosity and kindness were of note and little wonder that the prophet warned her of an imminent, impending famine that was coming upon the nation. The Prophet advised her to get out of the country for seven years to avoid the famine. This was a special privilege of looking after the man of God. She became privy to information that was confidential about the nation.

Even the king was not in the know of what the future held. Of a truth, God is no man's debtor. So she went away leaving behind all her belongings while

EVEN THE BIRDS WIL PAY

the famine was raging according to the instruction of the Prophet. After the famine was over, she came back to her nation to discover that all her belongings had been vandalised, and her estates occupied by other people who had encroached on all that she had.

This could have caused her great pain and worries. Some people would have even developed raised blood pressure realising how much was at stake.

She could even have involved the police in the recovery of her belongings, but as a wise woman, she refused to do any of such. She chose instead to approach the king who is the ruler of the nation to report her predicament. Instead of approaching the courts and engaging in physical war, let us approach the King of Kings on our knees and make our request known to Him.

Her choice of going to the king was so timely because it was the time of her restoration from heaven. It was a divine arrangement. Her case was already being discussed by the king and our good friend Gehazi. It was heavenly orchestrated, and without much labour, the king appointed an officer with a royal mandate that all the people that had encroached on her estate while she was away should vacate and restore all that was hers.

The restoration was to be very extensive and all-encompassing to the point that the mandate of the king was also to the effect that even the fruits that must have been taken or eaten from her vineyard must be fully restored.

This led me thinking that while this woman was away some of the fruits might have over ripened, and some birds may have decided to pick these fruits.

Therefore, if all the fruits had to be restored, then it is not only men that will have to pay for what they ate, even the birds will have to pay back what they wrongfully picked.

So when we talk about restoration we need to understand that it may not only be men that will and must pay back, 'EVEN THE BIRDS WILL PAY.'

Help will come from where you are expecting and from unlikely sources, help will come in Jesus name.

Let us approach our great God who has given his angels charge over our lives to restore all that the enemy has stolen from us, even to the point of things that we did not realise belonged to us.

EVEN THE BIRDS WIL PAY

Chapter 1

Restoration

When I tell people 'Even the Birds will pay,' some will think that I am speaking about restoring things that exist back to its original owner. While this is welcome, how would you explain the restoration of fruits that had been eaten and digested by the birds? 'Can those be restored back to me?' You might ask. Sure. This is the purpose of this chapter as we begin to explore the restoration we are talking about.

One major lesson I recently learnt is that I have such a superficial knowledge of the word 'Restoration.' You see, sometimes we overestimate our knowledge on many issues. So as I began to study the word deeply and intensely, I then realised that all I ever needed is encapsulated in restoration.

The word 'Restoration' stands for Repair, Refurbish, Refit, Mend, Recondition, Rehabilitate, Rebuild, Reconstruct, Remodel, Redecorate, Revamp, Makeover, Redevelop, Renovate, Modernise, Updates, Upgrade, Gentrify, Refurbish, and Facelift.

Depending on what you are going through at any particular time or season of life, there is a part of the restoration that applies to you.

Repair

For someone going through a stressful marriage or parenting, there is the possibility of the relationship to experience restoration as a form of REPAIR. Simply put, the word repair means something that was paired together but has found itself unpaired. It can be repaired or put together or brought to a state of unity from disunity, discord or division.

Restoration can repair what is damaged, stolen or molested. Do you know that marriages heading for the rocks can still experience miraculous turnaround through the mercies of God? Don't be too amazed or surprised to see 'The Prodigal Son' heading home. This is not impossible for the God of restoration who specialises in repairing what has been unpaired.

Refit

To other people, Restoration will connote refit. What comes to mind is the example of nuts and bolts that were in place to secure a structure, but for whatever reason, the nuts and the bolts are beginning to disconnect. There may be the need to refit it together in other to restore the strength of the structure. All this is to alleviate all forms of friction and animosity that may have caused the disengagement and bring in total restoration.

Mend

A Psalmist once described God as 'The Heart Ache Mender.' What an attribute! When restoration occurs to very broken hearts, maybe due to broken relationships, failed businesses and many other traumatic experiences, it is always a session of Mending. My prayer is that you will experience divine mending and divine visitation in every area of your life in Jesus name.

Refurbish

This is a very significant act of restoration. This happens when one brings out the new from the old. When God changes your situation and gives you a new name, He changes your testimony. This was exactly what God did in the life of Elizabeth in Luke1:36,

> "And behold, thy cousin Elizabeth, she hath also conceived a son in her old age, and this is the sixth month with her, who was called barren."

Because it's your season of restoration, God will change your name from barrenness to fruitfulness.

Recondition

It is when God sorts you out and places you in a much better condition than the one you are presently in. Imagine a man travelling from a hot African climate into a country like Russia where the weather is freezing most of the time; it is only appropriate for him to change his clothing on arrival in Russia to condition his body to the new environment. God will decorate you to function on the higher level to which He is taking you. Restoration is when God recondition you to becoming more relevant and more productive.

Redecorate

This is another definition of the word restoration; restoring every good thing that the enemy may have stolen. The decoration was initially perfect, but along the line, something happened that messed it up. God can redecorate and make it more beautiful than before.

Revamp

When something is just about to die, probably because of fatigue, exhaustion and depression, it needs revamping. That is exactly the intention of God at this time of restoration.

"But they that wait upon the LORD shall renew their strength; they shall mount up with wings as eagles; they shall run, and not be weary; and they shall walk, and not faint" (Isaiah 40:31).

Rebuild

It is very encouraging, and it gladdens one's heart to know that God can and wants to rebuild everything that is broken down in our lives and around us. He does it in a way that He restores it to its former glory. The dry bones in Ezekiel 37:1-11 were fully revived, and God has not changed. Hallelujah.

Makeover

To enhance and reveal the beauty of a house, a life which in time past was a cynosure of all eyes but which for whatever reason, the beauty was fading away, and losing its relevance and prominence. There may be the need for such to be given a complete makeover which connotes restoration. God will give you a complete makeover in this season of restoration in Jesus name.

Redevelop

One familiar term to builders is to redevelop a site project or a broken down wall. Most times when something is redeveloped, it is taking cognisance of all the problems and anomalies that were in the project when it was originally done and making reasonable efforts to bring out something more durable and glorious than its original design. God is a developer; He can redevelop whatever we are trusting Him to do.

Renovate

Building what has been damaged, restoring the forgotten glory. Haggai 2:8 said

> *"The glory of the latter house shall be greater than the former."*

Modernise

To bring into modern relevance. The outdated, outclassed and forgotten style is done away with. It is a new beginning. What a great God we serve!

Update

When you are restored, you will be upgraded to relevance, and you will become current and needed.

Restoration moves you up; it restores the years wasted and updates you to the new level of grace and mercy.

Upgrade

This is when God uses restoration to up your grade. He takes you higher, and you operate on another class, but this time its upper level. It's promotion that moves you to another level.

Gentrify

Architects and builders are so used to this word because it's the system of restoring a rundown area that has lost its value. The process to restore such a project is referred to as gentrification. When God restores you, He is just gentrifying you to His glory.

Facelift

When God restores the face that has dropped, tired, and worn out, He makes it look radiant and makes it shine. You will see things that are high and lovely. If this is your desire, receive such now in Jesus name.

I declare boldly under God that if you are broken, this is your season of mending. If for whatever reason you are unhappy, this is your season of joy. Whatever you are going through, if you need repair, God is a repairer and restorer. God will give you a facelift; you are being redeveloped, renovated, and you are being relaunched. For everything that was lost, it's your season of divine restoration.

Here is a definite confirmation to this in 2 Samuel 30.

The enemy struck while the men were away. David was caught up with the Amalekites. In the ears of David men, restoration meant something more than the ordinary because they recovered more than what was taken away from them at Ziklag. We need to remember that this gang of marauders were already invading other cities before they got to Ziklag and had already carted away many goods from those cities. So when David and his men overran the Amalekites, they recovered their wives and children and also took all the other booty that they had looted from other cities. This explains why David was able to send gifts to many people who did not even participate in the battle.

It is, therefore, imperative to believe God for more than what you have lost because it's your time of restoration.

The enemy is always trying to work against whatever God had done, but despite all his efforts, our God is more than enough.

Chapter 2

Change is Coming Your Way

L ife can be very challenging. I have always asked myself why life is a continuous struggle and battle for some people. It is a known fact that being born poor does not necessarily mean you have to fight through your existence, in the same way as being born with a silver spoon in the mouth, cannot in any way guarantee a stress-free life.

To be born poor is not a crime, but to die poor is the worst thing that can ever happen to a man.

Nothing is written in the laws of Persians and Medians that cannot be changed. Many wealthy people had died poor while many so-called poor people had died to leave behind a great legacy and wealth.

> *"I returned, and saw under the sun, that the race is not to the swift, nor the battle to the strong, neither yet bread to the wise, nor yet riches to men of understanding, nor yet favour to men of skill; but time and chance happeneth to them all"* (Ecclesiastes 9:11).

For you to experience restoration, there are certain things you must do.

Seek knowledge and apply wisdom

It can be very worrying when a king dies like a servant; like Abner, a man of great influence, who died like a fool. It is disheartening to observe many people led to eternal misery and regrets at the brink of their miracle, through foolishness and wickedness.

When you begin to notice an eagle mingling and feeling comfortable among chickens or a lion at peace walking and interacting with cats, it's nothing but an aberration, a misfit and a curse. Something somewhere must have gone wrong.

Many people are born with divine mental capacity and grace and are destined to become very great in life, yet they die unsung due to one thing or another. They die unrecognised and miserable. This needs to be seriously investigated.

In the Christian circle, we unjustly blame and apportion glory to our enemy, the devil. However, I believe that we should begin to learn the act of taking responsibility for some of our follies. Refusal to adequately apply wisdom and knowledge can bring untold hardship and sometimes result in fatal consequences.

Hosea 4:6 (NIV) brings out the point I am trying to make in a clearer sense.

"My people are destroyed from lack of knowledge. Because you have rejected knowledge, I also reject you as my priests; because you have ignored the law of your God, I also will ignore your children."

If someone is not well informed, they can end up being deformed. It is stated very clearly that, lack of knowledge kills. Satan is not to be blamed for all issues, but the lack of knowledge can lead to destruction. Information that is correctly processed and practised is a very great way out of destruction.

I recently heard a joke from a preacher who said that he had the opportunity of seeing the devil one day and to his greatest shock the devil was crying and completely frustrated. He then asked the devil the reason for his frustration. The devil said that Christians are responsible for his misery and went further to lament that, for everything that goes wrong with them, they automatically accused him; even for things that he has no clue about. He was so bitter that he was calling them liars and said that he is anxious about some lies that are being circulated about him.

I hope that none of us will die with all the potentials that are in us without releasing them in Jesus name.

I invest in shares and bonds, and from time to time I receive updates and dividend certificates. The certificate is to inform me that the money is mine. To be able to convert the certificates to cash in my bank account, all I need to do is visit any branch of my bank with them.

Ignorance of what to do has kept many people in poverty. Through ignorance or lack of effort, many companies are sitting on money that belongs to other people.

Many of our banks are reaping from where they never sowed as many deposits and fortunes of customers who may be dead without notifying their relatives of such investments automatically become part of the bank assets. It is not the responsibility of the bank to inform the relations of deceased clients due to confidentiality. As long as nobody makes an enquiry or ask any question about such investment, it is a loss to the family but a significant gain to the bank. Why make the rich bank richer undeservedly.

In one of my many visits to Switzerland, a friend of mine said that Switzerland can never be poor because many people from around the world will always bring their money for safe keeping and most of them will eventually forget the Personal Identification Number (PIN) when they fall into a coma. Most of them will not even disclose such investments to their family so when they eventually die; the investment automatically becomes part of the GDP of Switzerland. What a disaster!

There are several Characters in the pages of the scripture that we need to learn from. They were destined to be great. It looked like their paths were already laid in gold. Charting another path for their lives, some have ended up as disasters and an atrocious reference point. The story of one of such people is in 1 Kings 12. Starting from the very first verse, we read,

> *"Rehoboam went to Shechem, for all Israel had gone there to make him king."*

Initially, there were no oppositions and no rivalry against Rehoboam's rulership. He needed not to campaign. Everything seemed ready. The stage was already set for him to emerge as Israel's next King. He must have been looking forward to the day of his coronation. The family was already talking to the caterers for quotations. Musicians were already hired for the great day. Fashion designers must have been very busy in choosing colours, and the event planners must have had sleepless nights on how the party will be coordinated. What a sight! So much hope was in the air.

However, for all these to happen, there is a very simple, short and easy test to pass; a riddle to resolve

> *"³So they sent for Jeroboam, and he and the whole assembly of Israel went to Rehoboam and said to him: ⁴"Your father put a heavy yoke on us, but now lighten the harsh labour and the*

> *heavy yoke he put on us, and we will serve
> you." ⁵Rehoboam answered, "Go away for three
> days and then come back to me." So the people
> went away" (1 Kings 12:3-5).*

Let's take a more critical look at this situation. The people were not saying that they changed their plans neither were they saying that they were not prepared to serve Rehoboam, their new King. They were not even too bothered about carrying some burden. They just wished that he would consider making it lighter.

To a man of wisdom, who is not yet crowned, at least he should have considered giving the people hope; something they can look forward to. For a foolish person, a gesture that seems so straightforward and easy can still become so challenging and may lead to their downfall if not sensitively handled.

> *"⁵Rehoboam answered, "Go away for three
> days and then come back to me." So the people
> went away. ⁶Then King Rehoboam consulted
> the elders who had served his father Solomon
> during his lifetime. "How would you advise me
> to answer these people?" he asked. ⁷They
> replied, "If today you will be a servant to these
> people and serve them and give them a
> favourable answer, they will always be your
> servants" (1 Kings 12:5-7).*

He consulted with old men - tested, trusted, proven men - men who had seen it all. It is a known fact that anointing with experience guarantees longevity in ministry.

Look at the right and excellent counsel that was given to Rehoboam by the old men. They advised him of the need to be considerate and humane as a leader so as to win the people's heart and loyalty.

Leadership by coercion cannot last. See the foolishness of Rehoboam in contacting his colleagues for advice (1 Kings 12:8-11).

> *"8But Rehoboam rejected the advice the elders gave him and consulted the young men who had grown up with him and were serving him. 9He asked them, "What is your advice? How should we answer these people who say to me, 'Lighten the yoke your father put on us'?" 10The young men who had grown up with him replied, "These people have said to you, 'Your father put a heavy yoke on us, but make our yoke lighter.' Now tell them, 'My little finger is thicker than my father's waist. 11My father laid on you a heavy yoke; I will make it even heavier. My father scourged you with whips; I will scourge you with scorpions.'"*

The Bible was very clear on what this young man did. He foolishly rejected the counsel of the old men because it did not appeal to his pride. This advice seemed to undermine his authority, and for a young man who was aspiring to become the king, he felt the need to stamp his authority by force from the beginning. He thought that he needed all the respect that will make him feel like the one in control. He needed his ego bloated; he could not relate to a leader who wants to be a servant. So he dismissed sound counsel.

I have come to realise that when people consult you for counselling, they are usually predisposed to dismiss any counsel that does not appeal to them. Most times, the expectations of people during counselling is that you would rubber-stamp their own conviction even when it is clear that it's wrong.

Many marriages would have been saved but for the problem of pride, arrogance and ego. Humility makes someone accept a shortcoming than put on unnecessary arguments.

Rehoboam, the heir apparent, forsook the counsel of the old men and consulted with people that grew up with him. They were psychedelic, contemporary and trendy. They speak Queens English; are posh and fashionable. Though not tested, they were so arrogant and confident over nothing. They were craving for power, so they gave him counsel that was honest but lacked wisdom. They appealed to his ego and seemed to promote the spirit of domination.

It is unfortunate that many people cannot see beyond their noses. Rehoboam's young advisers forgot that the young man had not been crowned and that the staff of office was yet to be presented to him. They forgot that the people still had the power to change their minds. The coronation was still a proposal; it was not yet a reality. To them, the new king must come with force, cruelty and brutality so as to command respect.

Rehoboam's case merely confirmed Proverbs 13:20.

> "*20He who walks with wise men will be wise, but the companion of fools will be destroyed.*"

> "*16Now when all Israel saw that the king did not listen to them, the people answered the king, saying: "What share have we in David? We have no inheritance in the son of Jesse. To your tents, O Israel! Now, see to your own house, O David!" So Israel departed to their tents. 17But Rehoboam reigned over the children of Israel who dwelt in the cities of Judah*" (1 Kings 12:16-17).

What a shamble? The people changed their minds. Foolishness closed the gate on a great future. What a massive debt this silly boy must have incurred! The coronation that could have involved the entire nation was reduced to just two struggling tribes that had no choice but to tolerate the young insensitive King. With hopes dashed, and future blurred due laregely to inexperience, Rehoboam's subsequent action sufficiently proved how stupid the young man was.

> *"¹⁸Then King Rehoboam sent Adoram, who was in charge of the revenue; but all Israel stoned him with stones, and he died. Therefore King Rehoboam mounted his chariot in haste to flee to Jerusalem. ¹⁹So, Israel has been in rebellion against the house of David to this day"* (1 King 12:18-19).

This subsequent action proved that Rehoboam did not understand the magnitude of his decision by sending one of his foolish colleagues to go collect dues from people who had rebuffed his overtures as the king. This led to the fatal murder of the tax collector and Rehoboam's flight for his life, realising that the rebellion may lead to his untimely death. Can you imagine the price paid for stupidity?

The story of this young man is so touching as it actually may be the story of many people today. I usually refer to people of like stories as clouds without water; hopes that look very hopeful but suddenly turn into hopelessness.

It will be nothing short of regrets when something that seemed bagged suddenly slips out due to one's stupidity. Many people today are suffering the consequences of wrong decisions they have taken without proper counsel or of some stubbornness that has now resulted in a life of gloom and regrets.

Unfortunately, we cannot always run away from the consequences of our decisions which can be very devastating, and we do need divine grace and mercy to alleviate the long time effects.

Wisdom most often comes with age and experience. However, this may not always be true. The story of Gehazi teaches us not to accept counsel just because someone is older or more experience. It brings out the old prophet versus the young prophet syndrome. Let's read the story in 1 Kings 13:11-26.

> "*11Now there was a certain old prophet living in Bethel, whose sons came and told him all that the man of God had done there that day. They also told their father what he had said to the king. 12Their father asked them, "Which way did he go?" And his sons showed him which road the man of God from Judah had taken. 13So he said to his sons, "Saddle the donkey for me." And when they had saddled the donkey for him, he mounted it 14 nd rode after the man of God. He found him sitting under an oak tree and asked, "Are you the man of God who came from Judah?" "I am," he replied. 15So the prophet said to him, "Come home with me and eat." 16The man of God said, "I cannot turn back and go with you, nor can I eat bread or drink water with you in this place. 17I have been told by the word of the Lord: 'You must not eat bread or drink water*

there or return by the way you came.'" ¹⁸*The old prophet answered, "I too am a prophet, as you are. And an angel said to me by the word of the Lord: 'Bring him back with you to your house so that he may eat bread and drink water.'" (But he was lying to him.)* ¹⁹*So the man of God returned with him and ate and drank in his house.* ²⁰*While they were sitting at the table, the word of the Lord came to the old prophet who had brought him back.* ²¹*He cried out to the man of God who had come from Judah, "This is what the Lord says: 'You have defied the word of the Lord and have not kept the command the Lord your God gave you.* ²²*You came back and ate bread and drank water in the place where he told you not to eat or drink. Therefore your body will not be buried in the tomb of your ancestors.'"* ²³*When the man of God had finished eating and drinking, the prophet who had brought him back saddled his donkey for him.* ²⁴*As he went on his way, a lion met him on the road and killed him, and his body was left lying on the road, with both the donkey and the lion standing beside it.* ²⁵*Some people who passed by saw the body lying there, with the lion standing beside the body, and they went and reported it in the city where the old prophet lived.* ²⁶*When the prophet who had brought him back from his journey heard of it, he said, "It is the man of God who defied the*

*word of the Lord. The Lord has given him over
to the lion, which has mauled him and killed
him, as the word of the Lord had warned him.*

The young prophet was full of zeal and anointing;
a man who through prophecy caused the king's hand
to wither. Though young, he was a great prophet
with a great prophetic future. His naivety and lack of
ministerial experience made him a victim of priest
craft. He was conned by the old prophet, a master of
the game. The old prophet made it known to the
young prophet that he was a master of the game. His
ministerial exploits and testimonies intimidated the
young prophet. How can God leave me and speak to
you? This fact was daunting as the young prophet
insisted that he was following God's instruction, a
direct Word of God, which is reliable and consistent
in any given situation. The Old Prophet, on the other
hand, claimed that his leading was from an Angel. So
the folly of the young prophet was laid bare by
believing a man with so called 'angelic'
communication instead of the Word of God. What a
disaster!

This old prophet did not only terminate the
ministry and buried the future of the young, zealous
prophet; he also buried the young prophet's physical
body. No matter your spiritual height, you need to be
trained, so as to last in your journey.

Foolishness delay prayers

There was a friend who was trusting God for a marriage partner. He was a young manager with a very promising future working with an international firm. He was any woman's dream-come-true. There was this beautiful woman who had also been trusting God for a marriage partner. One day, my friend announced his intention of proposing to this sister on a particular Sunday and planned to do it immediately after the Church service. Since the Church was a large congregation and in order not to lose sight of this sister after the service, he decided to seat behind the sister during the Church service.

On the day, my friend was wearing a brand new shirt with very nice cologne and perfect hair cut in preparation for him to launch his manifesto. When the pastor announced that there was going to be a brief meeting with the women after the service, the sister disrespectfully muttered against the pastor. Unknown to her, this sister missed her opportunity of the proposal as my friend, who overheard her, was unsettled by her response. He felt concerned that if the lady could do that to her pastor, she may become uncontrollable at home. He took this as a warning from God.

What a shame! She came close to her miracle, but her character wrestled her to the ground. The last time we heard about this sister, she was still trusting God for a husband.

If you must expect restoration, if you desire the birds to pay, you need to pursue after knowledge acquisition and application of godly wisdom.

Chapter 3

Kill the flesh before it kills you

I feel the need to continue to emphasise the need to follow after godly counsel especially when it comes from people who have our best at heart. Much of the restoration we may be seeking may elude us if we refuse to live by God's standard and walk away from the divine plan and ignore godly counsel.

Samson could have avoided a lot of heartaches had he listened to the godly counsel of his parents. He instead chose to follow his fleshly desires and eventually died in the process though he seemed to have the world at his feet. The amazing surprise was that God used the situation to deliver Israel from the hands of the Philistines despite Samson's blatant rebellion.

There are several lessons to learn from the story of Samson and the Philistines. Please allow me to tell the story in my way.

I do not think there is any greatness and recognition more desirable than for heaven to delegate an Angel to announce the birth of Samson to his parents. Only a few people enjoyed this kind of privileged in the Bible; John The Baptist, and our Lord and Saviour Jesus Christ. Not even Apostle Paul.

The Angel gave Samson's parents very specific instructions on how to nurture and raise him. He was consecrated for a specific assignment

> "³And the angel of the Lord appeared unto the woman, and said unto her, Behold now, thou art barren, and bearest not: but thou shalt conceive, and bear a son. ⁴Now therefore beware, I pray thee, and drink not wine nor strong drink, and eat not any unclean thing: ⁵For, lo, thou shalt conceive, and bear a son; and no razor shall come on his head: for the child shall be a Nazarite unto God from the womb: and he shall begin to deliver Israel out of the hand of the Philistines" (Judges 13:3-5).

These instructions must be kept all the days of his life. Therefore it was the responsibility of Samson's parents to look after him when he was young. When he becomes mature, the responsibility will be his to obey God's instructions and ordinances. His actions had to be carefully guided knowing that he was such a special child. From the story, we could conclude that his parents kept their part of the deal.

> "²⁴And the woman bare a son, and called his name Samson: and the child grew, and the Lord

blessed him. ²⁵And the Spirit of the Lord began to move him at times in the camp of Dan between Zorah and Eshtaol" (Judges 13:24-25).

However, something went wrong when Samson became mature enough to make his own decisions.

"¹And Samson went down to Timnath, and saw a woman in Timnath of the daughters of the Philistines. ²And he came up, and told his father and his mother, and said, I have seen a woman in Timnath of the daughters of the Philistines: now therefore get her for me to wife. ³Then his father and his mother said unto him, Is there never a woman among the daughters of thy brethren, or among all my people, that thou goest to take a wife of the uncircumcised Philistines? And Samson said unto his father, Get her for me; for she pleaseth me well" (Judges 14:1-3).

The kind of women that pleased Samson were the Philistines, 'the forbidden tribe.' The parents noticed that Samson was beginning to go against the Nazarene vows they took, but all the pleas from his parent fell on deaf ears. Samson was more interested in satisfying his fleshly desires than the call of God upon his life.

God will invariably use this for His divine purpose. According to Romans 8:28,

> *"And we know that all things work together for good to them that love God, to them who are the called according to his purpose."*

> *"But his father and his mother knew not that it was of the Lord, that he sought an occasion against the Philistines: for at that time the Philistines had dominion over Israel"* (Judges 14:4).

God was still able to use this unfortunate situation for His glory. But there were so many warnings from heaven to help Samson overcome his demon. One of such warnings was when they were on their way to propose to this Philistine model. A strange lion suddenly appeared out of nowhere to threaten Samson, but instead for him taking heed, he was headstrong, and he went on to defy his Nazarene vow the moment he killed the Lion with his bare hands. A Nazarene was not supposed to kill or touch any dead thing. For a deeper understanding of what went wrong with Samson, we need to read a very profound analysis written by David Legge (2006). The rest of this chapter contains David's message.

Now we saw in our study of chapter 13 that Samson was a man of God, a Judge raised in Israel who started off with a promising start. We found that out as we looked at a couple of points that were illustrated for us in that chapter.

First of all, we figured out that Samson was a child of promise. In other words, first of all, he had a miraculous birth. His mother was barren, she was infertile, but God miraculously in a supernatural way allowed her to give birth to Samson because the nation needed a deliverer. Then we saw that he was a child of promise in the sense that he had many blessings, he was born with great potential and prospect.

Right before his conception, God had promised, through the Angel, that this would be the man who would begin to deliver Israel from the iron fist of the Philistines. In verse 24 we also read that *the woman bare a son, and called his name Samson: and the child grew, and the LORD blessed him*. As far as I'm aware, that's the only Judge that it is said that God blessed. So, this was a child of promise, and that's why Samson had a promising start. He had great prospects and potential for God.

We saw added to that fact was the family background that he had, and we found out in chapter 13 that he had very godly parents. They were parents who prayed for him; they also sought guidance from God regarding his upbringing.

So that added to Samson's promising start - not only his miraculous birth, and his many blessings, but the godly parents that brought him into the world and brought him up.

Then we saw that he was set aside as holy unto the Lord right from before his birth, for he was to be a Nazarite, the Angel told Manoah's wife. There were three vows that a Nazarite was under: first, his hair was to remain uncut; secondly, he was to refrain from the fruit of the vine; and thirdly, he was to touch no dead thing. We saw that that was the secret of Samson's strength: his separation from the world. We see that right early in his life, he was promising and showing great prospect because he proves himself in the service of the Lord in his home environment. God's power had come upon him, verse 25 of chapter 13 if you read it: 'The Spirit of the LORD began to move him at times in the camp of Dan between Zorah and Eshtaol'.

Right away we have a lesson here: when God chooses a man or indeed chooses a woman, He sets them apart for Himself like Samson. Here was a young man set apart to overcome the enemy. However, the tragedy was that Samson's enemy and God's enemy overcame him.

We learnt that Samson means 'sunlight', or 'sunny', and this young man ended his life in darkness, blinded by the enemy that he was supposed to conquer. We might well ask the question: how could someone like Samson, with such promise, such potential and prospect in life, descend to such a pathetic shadow of the man that God intended him to be?

Why should it be said of Samson, with such a promising start, that he messed it all up? Why should it be in our lives, with God on our side and all the blessings of God for us, that we should hit so many spiritual dead ends and come to nothing?

Now, my friends, I want you to see the stark reality of the parallels that are in the Christian life here – they're staring us in the face, and we need to see them. As Ephesians 1 verse 3 says, like Samson and his promising start, we are blessed with all spiritual blessings in heavenly places in Christ, everything is going for us; in the same way, Ephesians 1 and verse 4 tells us that we are chosen in Christ before the foundation of the world. We have been handpicked as Christians for God, and the reason Ephesians 1:4 gives us is that we should be holy and without blame before Him in love. The privilege of God's grace towards the Christian means that God has chosen us out of the world that is dying and damned, and we are set apart to be servants of God in holiness and separation from the world. Once we were slaves to sin, but God has taken us from being slaves to sin to servants of His holiness.

The choices that you will make will significantly affect your spiritual life, just as it did Samson's.

We see here that his downward spiral of breaking his consecration to God started when he rebelled against his parents.

That was Samson's primary problem in the home, and it's an issue in the home even today.

We read that, as the Lord Jesus' return comes nearer, 2 Timothy 3 verses 1 and 2 tell us that 'in the last days perilous times shall come. For men shall be lovers of their selves, covetous, boasters, proud, blasphemers, disobedient to parents, unthankful, unholy'.

This rebellion in Samson's life was evidenced first of all in his demanding attitude. In verse 2: 'he came up, and told his father and his mother, and said, I have seen a woman in Timnath of the daughters of the Philistines: now, therefore, get her for me to wife'. In verse 2 he says 'I have seen', and then he says later 'she pleaseth me well', and in verse 3 your margin should read that it means 'she is right in my eyes'. 'I've seen a girl, and she's right in my eyes, therefore get her for me!' You see that he's telling his parents what to do, he's not asking them for permission.

Is that not the spirit of the age today?

That is the mark of a materialistic, or a hedonistic society, a society that is drunk on pleasure, a society that has rejected the rule and reign of God. What you see in society is reflected in individual lives in a cameo, and we see people living like this: they are living by sight and not by faith. What they see, what they feel, they're living a sensual existence - and this was Samson's problem.

In the home, he was rebelling against his parents, and it's seen in his demanding attitude where he saw this woman - he began to walk by sight and not faith. As we go through Samson's life, we find that his eyes were one of his biggest problems. He couldn't control his eyes, he lusted with his eyes, and he was guided by his eyes rather than the law of the Lord.

We see it in chapter 14 verse 1: 'I have seen', he had seen a woman in Timnath. When we turn to chapter 16 and verse 1, 'Then went Samson to Gaza, and saw there a harlot, and went in unto her'. Verse 21 of chapter 16,

> *"But the Philistines took him, and put out his eyes, and brought him down to Gaza, and bound him with fetters of brass, and he did grind in the prison-house."*

His eyes were his problem, and eventually, his eyes would become his downfall, and he would lose all sight because of his sin through the eyes.

Well, Samson had great physical strength, at times he had great spiritual strength as the power of God came upon him - but when it came to women he had no strength, he had no control over his fleshly appetites.

The sexual urge is something very, very strong. If you do not control it, it will control you! Proverbs 6 and 27 tells us

> *"Can a man take fire in his bosom, and his clothes not be burned?"*

Many people today are ignited, completely consumed by lust - and I would say it's perhaps harder to protect yourself and be pure in this society today than it has ever been.

I wonder, have you got eye trouble? Well, 'eye trouble' is only the symptom of 'I trouble' - because Samson's principal problem was that he was not living to please the Lord, he wasn't even living to please his parents, he was living to please himself. It's seen in this demanding attitude: 'I have seen, she pleases me, she's right in my eyes, get her for me!'

Then secondly, his rebellion against his parents is seen in the unequal yoke, verse 3. His father and mother said: 'Is there not a woman among the daughters of your brothers, among all the people who you can take a wife? Why do you have to go to the uncircumcised Philistines?'.

Now, how many times has this scene been repeated in Christian homes down through the years?

'Mum, Dad, I've seen a girl, I want to marry her'.

'Great!' The parents say, 'Where does she worship?'

'She doesn't'.

'She doesn't? When did she become a Christian?'

'She's not'.

'Doesn't the Bible say, son...'

'I don't care what the Bible says! We're in love, and it doesn't matter what you say, what the Bible says, I'm going to marry her!'

The answer that came back from Samson is the answer that often comes back from our young people: 'Get her for me, she pleaseth me!'

Then we see secondly that Samson's downward spiral of broken vows took another step down when he renounced his vows in verses 5 to 9. He rebelled against his parents, and then he renounces his vows.

Samson renounced his vow of separation without actually renouncing it - did you get that? Samson renounced it without actually renouncing it - you go through this passage, you'll not find one place where he says: 'I'm going to start drinking wine now, I'm going to cut my hair, and I'm going to start touching dead things'. It came gradually, subtly, in a deceiving way.

There are many Christians and, like Samson, as far as anybody knows they're still obedient to their dedication and obligations to God - yet the inner symbols of their consecration are null and void, they're gone! Samson began to value his consecration to God less and less; he became comfortable with his broken vows without actually articulating it with his mouth.

Thirdly, here's another step downward: he made a joke of his behaviour, verses 10 to 14.

There is a problem, as a Christian, if we start to joke about sin, if we make fun of those trying to avoid sin and live holy lives, if we start to accept the world's caricature of what a Christian is, and we start to agree with them about how we view Christians - that's a problem.

This was a sign of Samson's backsliding: he treated his sin and the vows of holiness that were upon him flippantly. He talked about his faults and his backslidings frivolously. We see him at this wedding feast, perhaps, and he gives this riddle as an offering to his thirty companions. He says to them: 'If you get it right, you'll get thirty complete outfits, and if you don't get it, then I'll get the thirty linen garments and thirty changes of clothes'. The riddle is found in verse 14 if you look at it - it's simple when you know the answer!

In verses 15 to 18, when the men failed to guess, they went to Samson's wife and said: 'Persuade him to tell us, or we'll burn your father's home and all your family and your possessions'. She hounded him and nagged him, and eventually, he gave up the answer. In verses 19 and 20 we see that Samson lost the deal, and he had to go and kill thirty men to get the clothes.

We find that this sin is leading to more anxiety, more agony, and more tragedy in the life of this man Samson. He feasts with the Philistines; he associates with them more and more on a social basis. He begins to play riddles with them, and all the while, what was he disclosing? Not his strength as a man of God, but his weakness as a sinner!

Samson should have been out making war with the Philistines, but he was drinking wine with the Philistines, he was having a feast - and the only thing that could get him going to fight them was when his personal interests were at stake, and it was a spirit of vindictiveness that got him to get on his feet and to go and slay them. No longer was he fighting to uphold the glorious name of the Lord, but he was fighting to fulfil his will.

See it: God used this event to give Samson occasion to attack the enemy. He was going down to marry her, to bring them into his family, but because of this event and the sour way it went, Samson ends up in verse 19 of chapter 14 killing thirty men.

Then in chapter 15, the first five verses, we find that he burns up the enemy's crops and he slaughters a great number of Philistines in verses 7 and 8; in verse 15 of chapter 15 we see that he slays a thousand men.

Now Samson hadn't planned these things, but God worked them out just the same. My friend, you cannot run away from God, especially if you're a child of God! You try and do it your way; God will have His way, He will have the last laugh - the only tragedy will be: you will lose even what you thought you were going to gain in the world. For, when Samson returned, he lost the wife that he'd left his home for, and it was his companion who took her.

As a Christian, are you going to work with God or are you going to work against God? Either way, He will work what He wants - the big question is: whose side will you be on?

Samson had broken his vows, what a promising start! Where is your consecration today? Is it still on the altar, or does it need to be put there again?

It is very unfortunate that those that are destined to be kings end up a pauper, nobility needs to be nurtured to be maintained and sustained.

Once you make up your mind to marry a Philistine, it's just a matter of time before you reap the reward of disobedience. You can ask King Solomon and King Ahab. Despite their exploits and conquests, they had to bow their knees before strange gods. I am sure when these two great kings look back, it will be nothing but regrets and sorrow. Proverbs 31:30 (NIV)

> *"Charm is deceptive, and beauty is fleeting; but a woman who fears the Lord is to be praised."*

It is a common saying whosoever marries the devil's daughter automatically chooses the devil as his father in law. And I guess it is mandatory for the father in-law to pay his daughter a visit in her matrimonial home as often as possible. What a disaster and a future in jeopardy, a time bomb waiting to explode!

Furthermore, it is advisable to look at issues critically and assess the mistakes and reckless decisions that we may have made in the past and find the best ways to correct or amend some of these decisions and better still to appraise it as to avoid such pitfalls in the future. We need to overcome the problem of blaming other people and even the devil for our predicaments. The moment we cannot admit our wrongs, and we continually trade blames, it's a sign that one is not ready to progress in life. It's time we face the situation squarely so as to find a way out of our predicaments.

Let us stop playing the Adam and Eve game; God asked Adam what went wrong. He pushed the problem to Eve and Eve pushed the problem to the Serpent (Genesis 3:12-14). Thank God the Serpent was not allowed to explain its side; maybe he would have blamed the fruit, and the fruit may have blamed the tree, and the blame game will go on and on. We need to take responsibility and acknowledge our mistakes with the intention of rescuing our future.

Ananias and Sapphira needed not to die such a terrible way if not for wrong decisions and bad choices. We need to be very careful in taking some decisions in life.

The joy I have is that I don't know of any man who may not have made a wrong decision at a particular time, but the grace to acknowledge and seek every possible way to retrace, redirect and refocus is a step in the right direction.

Chapter 4

Mercy Prevailed

The wantonness and recklessness of Samson.

What stood out to me in the story of Samson is the beauty of the mercies of our God. We read in Judges 16:21-22,

> "²¹*Then the Philistines seized him, gouged out his eyes and took him down to Gaza. Binding him with bronze shackles, they set him to grinding grain in the prison. *²²*But the hair on his head began to grow again after it had been shaved.*

Samson's enemies thought they had finally conquered him, but mercy had a better plan for him. The hair that was shaven – Samson's symbol of power and authority – began to grow again. God had blinded the eyes of the Philistines not to notice this significant development. This is very encouraging to us all that the hair of grace and greatness that we may have lost due to ignorance, recklessness and stupidity

EVEN THE BIRDS WIL PAY

can and will grow again. This was a confirmation of the promise of God.

The Four Locusts

> *"And I will restore to you the years that the Locust hath eaten, the Cankerworm, and the Caterpiller, and the Palmerworm, My great army which I sent among you"* (Joel 2:25).

If it was a man that made this kind of promise, he might be sincere and genuine with his intentions, but issues may arise that were not initially taken into consideration, which practically, may make it impossible for the promise to be delivered. However, with God, there is only one certainty. God will never make any promise that He will struggle to achieve. This is confirmed in Psalm 89:34,

> *"My covenant will I not break, nor alter the thing that is gone out of my lips."*

His words carry integrity, and therefore you can count on it. It has never failed.

The picture painted in Joel 2:25 is such that the consequences of whatever we are going through may be down to what we have or have not done, yet the extent of the influence of the vast army of Locust is no longer under our control. We cannot exercise full control or take full responsibility for the degree to which the consequences are delivered.

We need a deeper understanding of the four agents of destruction mentioned in Joel 2:25.

The Locust

In another translation, it is referred to as the Swarming Locust, or better still, the Flying Locust. They are reckless, and the sight of any green leaf is a great attraction for them. They tend to take delight in destroying any good thing in sight. They fly to destroy the leaves of plants and can appear anytime.

These are Locusts that are spiritually responsible for laying waste all the strategy and plans one may have made for progress and try to render it unattainable and frustrated. They are spiritual barriers that cause spiritual upheavals whenever they attack.

The Cankerworm

These are also known as the Cleaving Locust. They cleave unto the leaves until there is nothing and will not let go until they have sucked the tree dry. They may not be easily noticeable or recognise, but their effects are massive.

The Caterpillars

These are otherwise known as the Stripping Locust. From the sound of their name, which is the actual representation of their actions, whenever they attack a tree, their intention is to strip the tree naked and open, making it unable to defend itself. They are dangerous creatures.

When this kind of locust is engaged in spiritual warfare, they tend to strip a man of protection and destroy all great and good things of life. They also destroy relationships and break down the health of the individual under attack. In fact, the person under attack will wish for rather death than continue to endure pain.

The Palmerworm

These are also referred to as the Gnawing Locust. According to the dictionary, this kind of Locusts bite and nibble persistently. They cause persistent distress and anxiety and can operate via many avenues. They are spoilers, destroyers and manipulators and can be very dangerous and tough to eradicate. According to Nahum 3:13,

> *"You have increased the number of your merchants till they are more numerous than the stars in the sky, but like locusts, they strip the land and then fly away."*

The primary assignment of these locusts is to strip the land and fly away, leaving you to face the consequences of their actions alone.

You will recollect that it was one of these agents that God used in Egypt to plunder the nation during the time of Moses. The Locust was commanded and permitted to eat all the good product and great things in the land. The best of the land was severely attacked by the Locusts, and it was another story entirely.

> *"4Else, if thou refuse to let my people go, behold, tomorrow will I bring the locusts into thy coast: 5And they shall cover the face of the earth, that one cannot be able to see the earth: and they shall eat the residue of that which is escaped, which remaineth unto you from the hail, and shall eat every tree which groweth for you out of the field: 6And they shall fill thy houses, and the houses of all thy servants, and the houses of all the Egyptians; which neither thy fathers, nor thy fathers' fathers have seen, since the day that they were upon the earth unto this day. And he turned himself and went out from Pharaoh. 7And Pharaoh's servants said unto him, how long shall this man be a snare unto us? Let the men go, that they may serve the Lord their God: knowest thou not yet that Egypt is destroyed?" (Exodus10:4-7).*

In its spiritual application, when locusts attack a man, the same effects of confusion, frustration and defeat will manifest. Life can be frustrating when someone is running in a circle. Man's only hope is God's promise of full restoration.

Just as the Book of Joel helped us to identify four major satanic agents in the form of locusts, in the Book of Zechariah, there are remarkable facts of four major satanic agents that we also need to understand to fully grasp the need and the way to receive our restoration.

For any revolution to take place, there must be people who are agitating and asking genuine, relevant questions.

It is imperative for us to know that nothing is made to last forever. All chemical and biological products must have the expiry date boldly inscribed on it. After such a date, the product may not be as potent and efficient as at the time of manufacture. In Genesis 27, Esau, while in crisis, was encouraged by his father that the yoke of Jacob on his head was not forever. So the day to the end of some of our challenges is here already.

Revolutions start with revelations. Before a man can engage in any meaningful action, he must first have an understanding of who he is, where he is and where he is going. We read in Judges 6:1-13 that before Gideon was able to defend Israel, he had an encounter with the God of revelation.

> "*1And the children of Israel did evil in the sight of the Lord: and the Lord delivered them into the hand of Midian seven years 2and the hand of Midian prevailed against Israel: and because*

of the Midianites the children of Israel made them the dens which are in the mountains, and caves, and strongholds. ³And so it was, when Israel had sown, that the Midianites came up, and the Amalekites, and the children of the east, even they came up against them; ⁴and they encamped against them, and destroyed the increase of the earth, till thou come unto Gaza, and left no sustenance for Israel, neither sheep, nor ox, nor ass. ⁵For they came up with their cattle and their tents, and they came as grasshoppers for multitude; for both they and their camels were without number: and they entered into the land to destroy it. ⁶And Israel was greatly impoverished because of the Midianites; and the children of Israel cried unto the Lord. ⁷And it came to pass, when the children of Israel cried unto the Lord because of the Midianites, ⁸that the Lord sent a prophet unto the children of Israel, which said unto them, Thus saith the Lord God of Israel, I brought you up from Egypt, and brought you forth out of the house of bondage; ⁹and I delivered you out of the hand of the Egyptians, and out of the hand of all that oppressed you, and drave them out from before you, and gave you their land; ¹⁰and I said unto you, I am the Lord your God; fear not the gods of the Amorites, in whose land ye dwell: but ye have not obeyed my voice. ¹¹And there came an *angel of the Lord, and sat under an oak which was in Ophrah, that pertained unto Joash the Abiezrite: and his son Gideon threshed wheat by the winepress, to hide it from the Midianites. ¹²And the angel of the Lord appeared unto him, and said unto him, The Lord is with thee, thou mighty man of valour. ¹³And Gideon said unto him, Oh my Lord, if the Lord be with us, why then is all this befallen us? And where be all his miracles which our fathers told us of, saying, did not the Lord bring us up from Egypt? But now the Lord hath forsaken us, and delivered us into the hands of the Midianites."*

Gideon questioned why things were not working for Israel if indeed God was with them. Why were things falling apart? The answer to the question and the solution to the problem was immediately given. When genuine questions are raised, then the solution is not far.

Four Horns and Four Carpenters

In the book of Judges it was Gideon that was asking the question, but in the book of Zechariah, it was an Angel that was asking a question that will lead to revolution.

"Then the angel of the LORD answered and said, O LORD of hosts, how long wilt thou not

have mercy on Jerusalem and on the cities of Judah, against which thou hast had indignation these threescore and ten years?" (Zechariah 1:12).

When the right questions are asked it seriously attracts the right answers. God had been angry with Israel for seventy years which was meant to be the expiry date of His anger, and the Angel who may have been observing the events got a grip of the situation and asked God about Jerusalem. The answer the Angel got was very encouraging because the time of divine restoration and visitation had come.

"You will arise and have mercy on Zion; for the time to favour her, yes, the set time, has come" (Psalm 102:13).

The time for God to favour, deliver and give you breakthrough, is now. If only you can trust that heaven is ready to shower on you the years that the locust and the other locust had eaten, you will begin to experience the God of now.

We can observe what heaven was waiting for from the question the Angel asked. In response to this question, heaven gave an explanation of why things went down for Israel as a nation.

In Zechariah 1:16, it was recorded that the main thrust of the issue was because God was angry with Israel. The heathen surprisingly took advantage of their predicament and helped further compound their misery. They took undue advantage of their calamity and exploited them far beyond the fair punishment for their shortcomings.

We need to understand that affliction and bondage are not meant to be forever even for the things done out of stupidity and for wrong decisions made. Borean Study Bible of 2 Corinthians 4:17 reads,

"For our light and temporary afflictions...."

All afflictions are meant to be temporary. What a great news for us all in Zechariah 1:16,

"Therefore thus saith the Lord; I am returned to Jerusalem with mercies: my house shall be built in it, saith the Lord of hosts, and a line shall be stretched forth upon Jerusalem."

When mercy speaks, judgment is terminated, afflictions are over, and the influence and dominion of Locusts are reversed. So it is a season of joy that calls for celebrations, and when such happen according to verse 17 of the passage, prosperity takes over from drought, lack and want. When restoration occurs comfort and peace become the order of the day, and that was what God promised the nation of Israel and anything short of this was not to be allowed.

One of the very striking issues on this restoration was the mention of the four horns. This reminds us of the four types of locust in the book of Joel. Why four again?

Going by the history of Israel as a nation, they had been through a lot, and they were surrounded by many hostile, contending neighbours and at that particular time, it was alleged that the four horns represented the Gentile nations that surrounded Israel namely Egypt, Assyria, Babylon and Persia. Anywhere Israel turned to was an enemy nation who prevailed over Israel because it was a backsliding nation. The solution for the survival of the nation of Israel was in restoration from Yahweh, and so when the restoration was announced, domination became practically impossible.

Whatever the enemy has destroyed or tampered with, God can restore. It was very encouraging in verses 20 and 21 to see the arrival of the four Carpenters. Their mission was to repair what had been damaged; to restore what had worn out and put the nation back on her feet. They are spiritual carpenters sent from heaven for our divine restoration.

For us, it is a welcome development and a sign of taking back what belonged to us. It is your time of restoration, the mercy of God has prevailed over judgement.

Four Evil Forces

Surprisingly, four other evil forces similar to the elements of destruction and agents of darkness of the Books of Joel and Zechariah appear in the New Testament. We can identify them as; Principalities, Powers, Rulers of darkness, and Spiritual Wickedness in heavenly places (Ephesians 6:12).

It is vital to note that this agreement by the three viewpoints that we have looked at proves to us that despite the attempts of the enemy to deceive us, his mode of operation is still very much the same. He may choose to hide and operate in diverse ways but the old foe is still the same.

Thanks be to our God who has given us the grace to overcome. The enemy may show up in several ways, but the name of Jesus is still an effective tool for dealing with it. Whatever way we choose to look at issues, spiritual warfare is real, but more importantly, the mercy of God is much more available and potent to overcome all the fiery darts of the enemy.

The fact that Jesus died and took our place on the cross to redeem us from death and its penalty is a sure guarantee of divine mercy. Jesus became sin so that we can become the righteousness of God. Therefore, if there is any race or people that are sure of receiving divine mercies, our generation is better positioned to access all the benefits of redemption. We can no longer allow the enemy free access into our lives. 2 Corinthians 5:17-18 declared,

> "*17Therefore if any man be in Christ, he is a new creature: old things are passed away; behold, all things are become new. 18And all things are of God, who hath reconciled us to himself by Jesus Christ, and hath given to us the ministry of reconciliation.*"

The word 'reconciled' connotes new beginnings; new relationships. It simply means that the slate is clean and it's a new day.

EVEN THE BIRDS WIL PAY

Chapter 5

You Can Leap Over a Wall

"For by thee I have run through a troop, and by my God have I leaped over a wall" (Psalm 18:29).

This is the testimony of King David. I honestly desire a private dialogue with King David for the insight into the number of walls he had to leap over in his little life as I try to list the few in scripture. Starting with the negative comments of his siblings, being alone with the sheep, the days he fought the bear and the lion, to the battle with Goliath. I would like to know what was going through his mind with King Saul chasing him to assassinate him, the Absalom revolt, the death of Ammon, the revolt of Joab, the insults and insinuations of Sheba, to count but few. Looking back, it's all nothing but a testimony to the glory of God.

Therefore, we can boldly declare that with God's mercy and faithfulness, the hardest and the tallest walls, will soon become our personal testimonies in Jesus name.

There are challenging situations of life that present themselves as walls. They always look impossible and daunting, and the mere sight or remembrance of them can be very upsetting. We discover such a wall in the life of King Hezekiah in 1 Kings 38:1-6.

Somebody rightly put the picture here into perspective. Hope was completely dead. How would you explain a situation when the Bible clearly stated that the sickness of the king was to result in death? While the king was pondering on the declaration, he must have thought that in such a very difficult situation, talking to the Prophet, who was meant to be the carrier of good news will be the next best thing to do. Yet before requesting to summon the prophet, the prophet appeared uninvited just to declare that there was no hope of recovery and that death was at the door.

I remember an incident similar to this in my life which happened about ten years ago. I wasn't feeling well, so I decided to visit my Doctor. After listening to my complaints, he became more frightened than I was. I remember him strongly advising me that if I ever felt such pain again, I should call for the ambulance because it can be fatal if urgent attention was delayed. I immediately became very scared and worried. I remember calling my General Overseer who I believe has spiritual authority over me and what a relief when I discussed the situation with him.

He sensed the worry and fear in my voice and asked me if I could manage to make it down to his house. I did, and on getting to his house, he took the time to pray for me. I was so shocked that despite my fear and the gloomy situation I painted to my General Overseer, he only prayed for about five minutes and he told me it was done. To the glory of God, the pain disappeared, and I didn't have to call the ambulance. That was a wall I had to overcome to the glory of God.

In the case of Hezekiah, calling the General Overseer at this point of his life is of little or no comfort at all. So what can be done? The Bible made us aware that it was a wall.

I think that David's testimony of scaling through walls at this point will look like a joke; considering the magnitude and the dimension of this particular wall. I salute the courage of the King to understand that the prophet was not God but a messenger of the God of mercy. It is also to the credit of the King that he realised that nobody could understand your pain as much as you who is passing through it. Therefore he is the only one that can adequately represent himself in the court of our God.

So Hezekiah faced his wall. He did not ignore it, neither did he take it for granted. He began to plead his case in the court of mercy.

When you table your case at the court of mercy, you will find help. There were two encounters with the merciful God in the New Testament.

When approached by a Syrophoenician Woman for help to heal her dying daughter, Jesus told her that it was against tradition to heal her daughter just because they were not Jews who were referred to as children seating at the table. The Jews had the privileged of divine healing. However, this woman who refused to accept defeat and give up easily was quoted as referring to herself and her daughter as dogs who don't mind to feed on the crumbs that fall from the table of the children.

Another encounter was when Jesus declared that he had not found such a faith even among the Israelite on the occasion of the healing of the Centurion servant.

From these two encounters, the demands of the people were met when they refused to give up. They were ready and therefore positioned themselves for their miracles.

For Hezekiah, mercy found him and intervened to bring restoration. The same prophet of doom became the prophet of gain, and God restored to him another fifteen years just like that.

I was also thinking about our father in the faith Abraham when he was negotiating with the Lord in

Genesis 18 over the issue of Sodom and Gomorrah. God's intention was to spare the city based on fifty righteous people, but surprisingly God was open to bargaining on His decision. Abraham started to bargain with God until they got to ten, then he stopped. He probably thought it was too ridiculous for a whole nation not to have ten righteous people. Interestingly, I am of the opinion that if Abraham persisted in asking God to consider fewer people, his request surprisingly might have been granted.

The mercies of God is overwhelming, abundant and sustainable.

EVEN THE BIRDS WIL PAY

Chapter 6

His Grace will Work for You

The grace of God is so mighty, and we need to understand that it is all encompassing and it is the faithfulness of God that guarantees us restoration.

Somebody argued that the birds need not pay back, as what they did to the orchard is what God ordained them to do, so in other words, pecking the overripe fruit of the great woman when she was away was their legal right guaranteed and allowed by God. In as much as I agree with this submission, it is also right to know that Isaiah 49:24-25.

> *"24Shall the prey be taken from the mighty, or the lawful captive delivered? 25But thus saith the Lord, Even the captives of the mighty shall be taken away, and the prey of the terrible shall be delivered: for I will contend with him that contendeth with thee, and I will save thy children."*

The prey of the mighty shall be taken away and even the lawful captive delivered. The captives that are lawfully bound shall be delivered irrespective of the judgement they deserved.

It is fascinating to note that the working of grace is so great. How can you explain what happened in Acts 16:26.

> *"And suddenly there was a great earthquake so that the foundations of the prison were shaken: and immediately all the doors were opened, and everyone's bands were loosed."*

We need to understand that it was not just Paul and Silas that were locked up in prison. Other prisoners were convicted criminals; maybe murderers and people who were on death row due to what they had done. These kind of offenders are referred to as "lawful captives." However, it was shocking to realise that after the earthquake, all the prison doors were opened and everyone's chain was loosed. These included the hardened criminals. This is grace at work. So, when we talk about restoration, even the things that we may not be expecting to partake of are covered under the mercy of God. In Acts 27:15-22, we noticed,

> *"15And when the ship was caught, and could not bear up into the wind, we let her drive. 16And running under a certain island which is called Clauda, we had much work to come by the boat: 17Which when they had taken up, they used helps, undergirding the ship; and, fearing*

lest they should fall into the quicksands, strake sail, and so were driven. ¹⁸And we being exceedingly tossed with a tempest, the next day they lightened the ship; ¹⁹And the third day we cast out with our own hands the tackling of the ship. ²⁰And when neither sun nor stars in many days appeared, and no small tempest lay on us, all hope that we should be saved was then taken away. ²¹But after long abstinence Paul stood forth in the midst of them, and said, Sirs, ye should have hearkened unto me, and not have loosed from Crete, and to have gained this harm and loss. ²²And now I exhort you to be of good cheer: for there shall be no loss of any man's life among you, but of the ship."

Paul was on the ship with a set of criminals, and when the tempest was becoming so strong, the criminals would have thought that Nemesis had finally caught up with them and that they were about to pay for all the evil they had done before.

In the revelation given to Apostle Paul, the fact that they may have been condemned by people was conclusive, but God had not written them off. This is what is being described in the Bible as saved by grace.

"For by grace are ye saved through faith; and that not of yourselves: it is the gift of God: which is a gift from God" (Ephesians 2:8).

Salvation is an undeserved and an unmerited gift; God decides in His infinite compassion to have mercy on whom he will have mercy Romans 9:15.

> *"For He saith to Moses, I will have mercy on whom I will have mercy, and I will have compassion on whom I will have compassion."*

So restoration is a work of grace, and because we were born again by grace, it is our privilege to experience restoration in all areas of our lives. We would not continue to live in self-pity. We would not allow our enemy to continue to oppress us due to ignorance of the finished work of Christ on the cross. Simply put, we are saved by grace, and we live by grace, and we shall be ultimately saved by His grace. The grace of God has covered things that we had done in ignorance that we are not to be capable of remedying by ourselves.

Turning weakness into strength

There was once a Bible Salesman who was the best in his company. However, he was a very bad stammerer. He outperformed all of his colleagues who were more prolific speakers. One day his boss asked him, "How do you sell so many Bibles with this stammering of yours?" He replied "First I ask them if they want to buy a Bible. If the answer is no, I offer to read it to them for free. As I start to read my obvious stammer kicks in and they end up stopping me and offering to buy the bible and read it themselves to save their time."

EVEN THE BIRDS WIL PAY

Chapter 7

There is hope for you

There may be benefits and dues that you may not be aware have been hidden away from you. When the birds pay, those hidden benefits automatically come to you with interests as soon as God exposes them.

Recently, here in the UK, there was a television and radio advert prompting people to claim Payment Protection Plan (PPI) refund. It was such that if you had taken a loan or have opened some bank account in six years before 2001, the government decided to penalise the banks who at the time added PPI as part of the account opening or loan repayment.

Many people started claiming. All you needed was to give a Claim Company your name and account details. It was their duty to find out if you were eligible to claim.

For me, I never thought I was in any way eligible because the only loan I ever took from the bank was £5000 which I paid a few years later. I even remember when I was paying back to ask the bank to remove

PPI from the loan and I paid back the actual sum borrowed. I was so reluctant to apply. But one day, I just decided to try and apply for PPI refund as there was no penalty for applying. The worst that could have happened was for them to reply with a no. So I decided to phone one of the claim companies providing my details.

I received a cheque for an amount of £2400 after a few weeks of applying. It was such a shock that I could not believe it. The claim company succeeded in calculating what was due to me and they also sought for accrued interest which they successfully claimed on my behalf. I was never aware that I qualified for PPI refund, nor was sure that I was to receive back nearly half of the original loan I took. What a surprise?

I owned a few houses in the UK that were purchased as investments. I had never been lucky in the choice of tenants that rented my properties. Many times, they ended up not paying for months, and since the houses were on mortgages, I normally would use my savings to pay for the mortgages. It got so bad that I had to sell all of the properties so as not to go bankrupt. There was this particular tenant who was staying in one of my apartment. She was having issues with her finances, and she was not able to pay her rent. So I had to find a way to evict her from the property and told her not to bother about her rent arrears. She was thankful and moved. Since she left, I lost contact with her.

Surprisingly one morning, as I was washing my car right in front of my house, I just noticed a young woman greeted me. I could not recognise her, but she greeted me so warmly and was happy see me. She then asked if I could recognise her, but I said I could not. She then asked me if I owned property on a particular street and I said yes. Then she reminded me she was my former tenant who was owing so much. She apparently had been looking for me without success. Things were now okay with her finances, and she was not going to continue to owe me as she could understand I must have been struggling to pay the mortgage on the house then.

I thanked her and reassured her that there were no bad feelings held against her. I also made her realise that the mortgage had since been paid and I had no recollection of how much it was, so she is free to go. To my greatest shock, the young woman remembered how much she owed, and she insisted on paying the debt even after I told that her not to worry about it. We exchanged contacts, and she left.

About two weeks after, on getting to my front door, I noticed a big envelope addressed to my name and on opening it, I found a letter of appreciation from the same woman the full payment of the money she owed. What a marvellous God!

When the birds pay, even those that owe you will be blessed to pay you. God will convict their hearts to the point that they will be willing to pay up. These testimonies make Job 14:7-9 a reality in our lives.

> *"⁷For there is hope for a tree. If it is cut down, that it will sprout again, and that its tender shoots will not cease. ⁸Though its root may grow old in the earth, and its stump may die in the ground, ⁹yet at the scent of water it will bud and bring forth branches like a plant.*

You are worth more than a tree, and the book of Job makes us know that even for an ordinary tree there is hope. Then I like to let you know that there is hope for you.

There are a few reasons why people may decide to cut down a tree. It may be that it is occupying too much space or that no one receives benefits from the tree. Cutting down a tree may not necessarily end its life.

The Good News Bible (GNB) puts the Job 14:7-9 passage in a better perspective,

> *"⁷There is hope for a tree that has been cut down; it can come back to life and sprout. ⁸Even though its roots grow old, and its stump dies in the ground, ⁹with water it will sprout like a young plant."*

If you look at the old root of a tree and you also see that the stump is practically dead, you may be forced to conclude that nothing can happen again. But if you could hold on and decide to water it, and allow it a passage of time, it will bud and sprout again.

I often wonder why people give up so quickly. Hope makes faith work, while fear and doubt work together. If you live in doubt, you will experience fear, but if you live in hope, you will be positive and willing to exercise faith. The unfortunate thing about fear is that it hinders and debars us from experiencing the fullness of God's promises. A double minded man shall not receive anything from the Lord.

> *"⁶But let him ask in faith, with no doubting, for he who doubts is like a wave of the sea driven and tossed by the wind. ⁷For let not that man suppose that he will receive anything from the Lord; ⁸he is a double-minded man, unstable in all his ways" (James 1:6-8).*

I do not doubt that there are some very challenging cases in this world. Some are very pathetic, and there are times that I do not envy being a pastor because it can be somewhat overwhelming when you hear the stories of many people.

I remember a particular case I handled some years ago in Nigeria. One afternoon while counselling and praying inside the church I attended at the time, a woman approached me to tell of her challenges. She had been to the hospital and doctors could not diagnose her problem. She went to many religious places seeking for help but all to no avail. She also mentioned that she had visited a few churches in search of a permanent solution to the problem. So she heard about our deliverance service. That was why she came.

She narrated that she sometimes feel a particular movement in her tummy for weeks and whenever there was a movement, she would begin to hear the sound of a bird right inside of her crying so loud. Honestly, I started to think in my heart who the wicked fellow was that directed her to us for deliverance. Judging by the magnitude of her problem it was too late to regret.

I had not handled a case like hers before and did not know how to pray or what to pray for. I told her to stand up, and I laid my hand on her and began to speak in tongues. I did not know what to expect, but as I began to pray, I saw that she began to vomit. Upon close examination, I discovered that she was vomiting something like raw flesh. I was so shocked and at the same time excited that God would do what no man could do. I continued to pray until she stopped vomiting. That was the end of this particular case.

She was a Muslim but she gave her life to Christ, and she began to share the testimonies of God's faithfulness in her life.

I quote a famous preacher here in England who says "It is not over until it's over." I want to agree with this quote as I have seen God move in miraculous ways restoring joy and hope in many situations.

I was invited to preach alongside a renowned Nigerian evangelist some years ago. It was a weeklong open air crusade, and the programme was planned in a way that I was meant to minister after this great preacher noted for many signs and wonders. I asked the crusade organisers to reorder the programme for the evangelist to minister after me. I quietly asked for it to be rearranged because I knew if people witnessed great move of the Holy Spirit before I mount the podium, they would be looking forward to a greater manifestation when it was my turn. I did not want them to be disappointed. My host refused my proposal and said the Holy Spirit wanted it that way. I, therefore, warned them of the consequence of their action in case nothing tangible occurs when I minister.

On the day that the renowned Evangelist ministered at the crusade, there was such a mighty outpouring of the Spirit of God, and this put me in an awkward position. I decided to fast on the day until after the crusade night but I could not fast beyond 12:30 pm, so I decided to depend on the Holy Spirit.

In the evening of the crusade, the crowd was bigger than previous days as I had earlier predicted and I was introduced as the preacher for the night. My message was titled *"The God that answereth by fire."* It was a good message, but as I was rounding up, I told the audience that anyone hard of hearing and deaf should step out for prayers. It was as if the words fell from my mouth. I felt like recalling every word, but it was too late. However, I consoled myself that the deaf would not have heard what I said anyway.

Little did I know that there were four people in the crowd who were confirmed deaf and they were ushered to the pulpit. I was shocked, confused and did not know what to do. I reached out, laid hands on them one after the other but to confirm my expectation, nothing happened. I was about to dismiss them when I had a prompting in my spirit to lay my hand on their ears and pray. I quickly obeyed, went back to the first person, laid my hand on his ears and prayed. As I finished praying and removed my hands, he began to shout because he could hear. I was so shocked and encouraged. So I went to the second person, his hearing was restored, and so was the third person. Oh, you should have seen the excitement on everyone's faces. The last person's hearing was not restored, and I cannot explain why. He was unable to hear, but I was thankful for the other three who had their hearing restored.

Lazarus was dead for four days and by the knowledge of science, the situation is irreversible. It was such a hopeless situation that even the instruction given by Jesus to have the stone rolled away was considered very unintelligible. It was a revelation that despite this very challenging situation Jesus was still asking that the crowd believe. He was saying exercise hope, even in this hopeless situation.

I know now that my case is not hopeless. If Jesus can raise Lazarus that had been dead for four days, then there is hope for me. I am not yet dead, nor have I been buried for even a day. If Lazarus can rise, then I can rise. If Elizabeth and Zechariah could have children at their old age, then there is hope for me. I believe and stand on His promises and against hope just like that of father Abraham; I choose to walk in hope.

Do you believe God can restore back to you everything that you have lost; including those the birds had eaten? I do.

EVEN THE BIRDS WIL PAY

Chapter 8

The Attitude to Restoration

In order to raise our altitude in life, by which I mean, progress in life, there may be the need to change our attitude. To access what lies ahead of me, I may not have the power to change any other person, but I have the power and the ability to change myself if I so desire.

Many people are waiting for things to physically change before they are prepared to change their confessions. However, from the pages of the scriptures, I realise that faith is not in waiting; faith is in acting and believing God to bring to pass what he had earlier promised.

In the Book of Hebrews, the eleventh chapter revealed how the elders in the faith obtained the promises of God. In fact, the sixth verse stated that without faith it is practically impossible to please God.

> *"1Now faith is the substance of things hoped for, the evidence of things not seen. 2For by it the elders obtained a good report. 3Through*

faith, we understand that the worlds were framed by the word of God so that things which are seen were not made of things which do appear. ⁴By faith Abel offered unto God a more excellent sacrifice than Cain, by which he obtained witness that he was righteous, God testifying of his gifts: and by it, he being dead yet speaketh. ⁵By faith Enoch was translated that he should not see death; and was not found, because God had translated him: for before his translation he had this testimony, that he pleased God. ⁶But without faith it is impossible to please him: for he that cometh to God must believe that he is and that he is a rewarder of them that diligently seek him" (Hebrews 11:1-6).

We learnt from Abraham and Sarah that you do not need to physically see the evidence of being pregnant before you change your name and your attitude.

"For what saith the scripture? Abraham believed God, and it was counted unto him for righteousness" (Romans 4:3).

What lessons can we learn from a woman like Hannah? She was accused of being drunk by Eli, whom I call 'the backsliding prophet.' Eli had lost his relationship with God so he could not understand the plight of this woman. Without asking Hannah any question about her prayer request so that he could offer counselling or any spiritual help, Eli decided to dismiss 'this nuisance of a woman.'

> "¹²And it came to pass, as she continued praying before the Lord, that Eli marked her mouth. ¹³Now Hannah, she spake in her heart; only her lips moved, but her voice was not heard: therefore Eli thought she had been drunken. ¹⁴And Eli said unto her, How long wilt thou be drunken? Put away thy wine from thee. ¹⁵And Hannah answered and said, No, my lord, I am a woman of a sorrowful spirit: I have drunk neither wine nor strong drink, but have poured out my soul before the Lord. ¹⁶Count not thine handmaid for a daughter of Belial: for out of the abundance of my complaint and grief have I spoken hitherto. ¹⁷Then Eli answered and said, Go in peace: and the God of Israel grant thee thy petition that thou hast asked of him. ¹⁸And she said, Let thine handmaid find grace in thy sight. So the woman went her way and did eat, and her countenance was no more sad. ¹⁹And they rose up in the morning early, and worshipped before the Lord, and returned, and came to their house to Ramah: and Elkanah knew Hannah, his wife, and the Lord remembered her" (1 Samuel 1:12-19).

To my greatest surprise, Hannah chose to believe the words of this prophet and decided to change her attitude and trusted that her prayers were already answered. What an amazon of a woman of faith.

To further buttress my point on the need to change your attitude so as to prepare for restoration, we need to look closely at a major family from the pages of the scriptures. Their lives and stories are relevant to us today.

> "¹⁵And Laban said unto Jacob, Because thou art my brother, shouldest thou, therefore, serve me for nought? Tell me, what shall thy wages be? ¹⁶And Laban had two daughters: the name of the elder was Leah, and the name of the younger was Rachel. ¹⁷Leah was tender-eyed, but Rachel was beautiful and well favoured. ¹⁸And Jacob loved Rachel; and said, I will serve thee seven years for Rachel, thy younger daughter. ¹⁹And Laban said 'it is better that I give her to thee than that I should give her to another man: abide with me.' ²⁰And Jacob served seven years for Rachel, and they seemed unto him, but a few days, for the love he had to her. ²¹And Jacob said unto Laban, Give me my wife, for my days, are fulfilled, that I may go in unto her. ²²And Laban gathered together all the men of the place and made a feast. ²³And it came to pass in the evening, that he took Leah his daughter, and brought her to him; and he went in unto her. ²⁴And Laban gave unto his daughter Leah Zilpah his maid for an

handmaid. ²⁵And it came to pass, that in the morning, behold, it was Leah: and he said to Laban, What is this thou hast done unto me? Did not I serve with thee for Rachel? Wherefore then hast thou beguiled me? ²⁶And Laban said It must not be so done in our country, to give the younger before the firstborn. ² Fulfil her week, and we will give thee this also for the service which thou shalt serve with me yet seven other years. ²⁸And Jacob did so, and fulfilled her week: and he gave him Rachel his daughter to wife also. ²⁹And Laban gave to Rachel his daughter Bilhah his handmaid to be her maid. ³⁰And he went in also unto Rachel, and he loved also Rachel more than Leah and served with him yet seven other years. ³¹And when the Lord saw that Leah was hated, he opened her womb: but Rachel was barren" (Genesis 29:15-31).

It was the story and the love of Jacob and Rachel that made the headlines. Racheal happened to be the junior sister of Leah.

For Jacob to have served for another seven years in the name of love tells a story of how remarkably beautiful Rachel must have been.

The story was becoming so romantic and too good to be true. Quite unfortunately, there was a big challenge awaiting these two love birds that they were not in any way prepared for. On the very night of their wedding, there was an exchange, Leah for Rachel. This act bothered me and made me begin to ask some questions about the sisters. How come things were like these? Where were Rachel kept that night? Laban did not inform Leah of his intention beforehand. When Leah realised what was going on, she could still try to save the situation by bailing herself out of this embarrassing deceitful arrangement. However, Leah never raised any objection, peradventure!

The consequence of this arrangement was such that it caused very bitter rancour between the sisters. I wonder what Leah would have said to her younger Sister in subsequent days.

Jacob did not hide his complete disgust and total disrespect for Leah after he realised what happened the night before. Unfortunately, this attitude of Jacob was so glaring that even Heaven testified that she was hated.

So here, we are presented with three principal actors who were victims of their situation; people who were hurting inside, deeply wounded.

Leah

A woman who had not experienced much love, a reject, arguably not due to any fault of her own. She was adjudged to have weak eyes.

> *"Leah was tender-eyed, but Rachel was beautiful and well favoured" (Genesis 29:17).*

We need to realise that she did not create herself, so she had little or nothing to do to change her looks permanently.

Rachel

Rachel was a hardworking woman who went to the Well; a great woman that seemed to combine hard work with beauty. She was not the first born, and though she was beautiful, the tradition was hostile to her. She could not, and she was not free to marry whenever she wanted due to the tradition that made it compulsory for her elder sister to marry before her.

Jacob

A man that could not explain why his father would not bless him because he was not the firstborn. Customs and tradition played him out of destiny. He was on the run from his brother and here found himself trying to put together his future. He chose to serve for seven years to marry Rachel. It was at this point that he realised that deceit had different levels. How can a master in the game of deceit be simply deceived without noticing? He woke up the next morning to discover that the person that slept in his bed was not Racheal but Leah. After complaining, he was asked against his will to respect the tradition and serve another seven years to realise his ambition of eventually marrying Rachel. Jacob ended up becoming a polygamist even when he was not mentally prepared for this.

As the story unfolds, many other issues began to rear their ugly head.

> "31And when the Lord saw that Leah was hated, he opened her womb: but Rachel was barren. 32And Leah conceived, and bare a son, and she called his name Reuben: for she said, Surely the Lord hath looked upon my affliction; now, therefore, my husband will love me. 33And she conceived again, and bare a son; and said, Because the Lord hath heard I was hated, he hath therefore given me this son also: and she called his name Simeon. 34And she conceived again, and bare a son; and said, Now this time will my husband be joined unto me, because I have born him three sons: therefore was his name called Levi. 35And she conceived again, and bare a son: and she said, Now will I praise the Lord: therefore she called his name Judah; and left bearing" (Genesis 29:31-35).

For reasons beyond Jacob's control, Leah began to give birth whereas Racheal, despite all the love and attention, was barren.

Leah, realising all that had happened decided to fight her battle the best way she thought, and that was to use her babies naming ceremony as occasions to voice out her frustration and depressions. That was why she named her first son REUBEN meaning 'because the Lord hath looked on my affliction, now my husband will love me.'

It was challenging to see any link between this particular boy and the name given to him, but it's all to do with Leah and her predicament. Just imagine this boy in school, and his classmates decide to ask him for the meaning of his name, and his response was 'that my husband will love me.' I can just see the confusion on the faces of everyone. Reuben was being made to pay for a problem he did not create or understood.

Having used Reuben's name to negotiate for love, the question that came to my mind was, 'Did this action produce any positive result'? Of course not. So Leah resulted in naming her second son Simeon as another bargaining asset.

SIMEON means 'because God knows that I am hated.' How deceived is this woman called Leah? What on earth has this got to do with the destiny of this boy, or how can he explain his name to his colleagues? I have argued that it is never a good thing to allow whatever we are going through to have the power to define our lives.

"*Let the weak say I am strong and let the poor say I am rich*" is a line from a popular song taken from Joel 3:10. We need to do this not because the situation has changed but we may have to operate like God that calls those things that are not as if they were, knowing fully well that God is too faithful to lie.

Leah conceived again. What a grace to just conceive without any stress. Unfortunately, Leah refused to learn any lesson from her past actions, so she decided to name the child LEVI meaning 'now my husband will be joined to me seeing I have given birth to three boys for him.' She must have so reasoned that if Reuben birth did not produce the much-desired love from her husband and the birth of Simeon refused to change the attitude of Jacob, the birth of Levi the third child was a sure banker; a game changer that will make her husband be joined to her.

Quite unfortunately, this expectation was never a reality. The fact remained Jacob loved Rachel but tolerated Leah.

How many times in our present world do we try to work things out of our volition or power but many times it does not always add up.

Going forward, I am of the opinion that Leah had learnt her lesson in a tough way and she decided to give up her pursuit of attention. When she gave birth to the fourth boy, she decided to name him JUDAH meaning 'now will I praise the Lord.' Wow! What a change of focus and attitude? She seems to have learnt a very great lesson at this juncture of her life. It is only a fool that continues to do the same thing the same way and expect a different result.

She realised that waiting for things to change, going through life with scars and regrets is a short route to living an unfulfilled life of depression. She realised that Jacob's attitude towards her had not changed a bit. It was her decision to experience breakthrough that led her to choose the name Judah, 'PRAISE.' What a revelation? This revelation is what put paid to Habakkuk 3:17-19 (KJV).

> "[17]Although the fig tree shall not blossom, neither shall fruit be in the vines; the labour of the olive shall fail, and the fields shall yield no meat; the flock shall be cut off from the fold, and there shall be no herd in the stalls: [18]Yet I will rejoice in the Lord, I will joy in the God of my salvation. [19]The Lord God is my strength, and he will make my feet like hinds' feet, and he will make me to walk upon mine high places. To the chief singer on my stringed instruments."

Joy is personal; it should not be based on situations, circumstances, and occurrences.

This name makes us see that she encouraged herself in the Lord her God just like King David in 1 Samuel 30:6b;

> *"But David encouraged himself in the Lord his God."*

Leah shifted her focus from the problem and began to give sacrificial praise. It was so scary and sad to find out that in the history of the children of Jacob, the first three boys, Reuben, Simeon and Levi, whose destinies were used to bargain for love and attention, were eventually cursed by their father because the seed of confusion and hatred had been sown from their birth. The damage, abuse and neglect over the years had taken their toll. No wonder it was the lineage of Judah that produce the Messiah Jesus Christ.

There is a lot more to learn from the chapter following.

> *"1And when Rachel saw that she bare Jacob no children, Rachel envied her sister; and said unto Jacob, Give me children, or else I die. 2And Jacob's anger was kindled against Rachel: and he said, Am I in God's stead, who hath withheld from thee the fruit of the womb?"* *(Genesis 30:1-2).*

This was what exposed us to the level of rivalry, bitterness and rancour that had engulfed the family of Jacob. Here we see a very envious, aggressive Rachel who started to blackmail Jacob on her barrenness, and of course, the frustrated Jacob who was so angry that he ended up throwing punches at God Who behind the scene decided to close the womb of Rachel.

Things were so bad to the extent that Rachel was bent on having children by any means, even if it meant giving her maid as a surrogate mother to Jacob.

When the maid became pregnant and was delivered of a boy, it provided Rachel with an opportunity and weapon to fight her battle. It was a means to revenge Leah's humiliation over the years and can you imagine the name of the boy DAN.

> *"³And she said, Behold my maid Bilhah, go in unto her; and she shall bear upon my knees, that I may also have children by her. ⁴And she gave him Bilhah her handmaid to wife: and Jacob went in unto her. ⁵And Bilhah conceived, and bare Jacob a son. ⁶And Rachel said, God hath judged me, and hath also heard my voice, and hath given me a son: therefore called she his name Dan" (Genesis 30:3-6).*

Exactly the same old game by Leah that had yielded no tangible result. Names are significant as they are connected to the bearer's destiny in life. The name 'Dan' has no bearing on this boy's future; not in any way. It only had something to say about Rachel alone; not even about the surrogate mum.

Surprisingly, the maid became pregnant again, and for Rachel, this was an excellent opportunity to show how bitter she was about her older sister. To demonstrate her predicament, she decided to name him NAPHTALI meaning 'with great wrestling have I wrestle with my sister, and have prevailed.'

> "*7And Bilhah Rachel's maid conceived again, and bare Jacob a second son. 8And Rachel said, With great wrestlings have I wrestled with my sister, and I have prevailed: and she called his name Naphtali meaning 'God hath judged me and hath also heard my voice'" (Genesis 30:7-8, italics mine).*

I desire to ask questions about the youthful days of this particular boy. He must have been a wrestler in school noted for violence and strife. The foundation to this problem must have been because of the name given to him at birth. What a damage, and a way to start life!

Can you imagine the tension that existed within this family? Little wonder why Joseph's brothers did not blink an eye to sell Joseph as a slave because the seed of discord, disagreement and hatred had been sown earlier in their young lives. Can you imagine the memories that these names carried every time the mothers were calling the children names?

For Leah, she seemed to have learned her lesson and moved on in life. This explained the fact that when she also decided to give her maid to Jacob and a baby was born; she decided to name him GAD.

> "⁹When Leah saw that she had left bearing, she took Zilpah her maid and gave her Jacob to wife. ¹⁰And Zilpah Leah's maid bare Jacob a son. ¹¹And Leah said, A troop cometh: and she called his name Gad. ¹² And Zilpah Leah's maid bare Jacob a second son. ¹³And Leah said, Happy am I, for the daughters will call me blessed: and she called his name Asher" (Genesis 30:9-13).

Gad means 'a troop cometh.' Again, nothing to do with her situation; not even trying to implicate Jacob nor Rachel in the struggle.

Zilpah's other boy was named ASHER meaning 'a happy day.' She found joy deliberately in the midst of the struggles. She deliberately decided to put all the issues behind her so as not to further complicate the future and the destiny of her children. Look at her response of Leah in Genesis 30:14.

> *"14And Reuben went in the days of wheat-harvest, and found mandrakes in the field, and brought them unto his mother, Leah. Then Rachel said to Leah, Give me, I pray thee, of thy son's mandrakes. 15And she said unto her, Is it a small matter that thou hast taken my husband? And wouldest thou take away my son's mandrakes also? And Rachel said. Therefore he shall lie with thee tonight for thy son's mandrakes" (Genesis 30:14-15).*

This incident gave us the true insight into what was happening within the household. It seems like the dream of love and acceptance from Jacob was no longer a do or die affair, so she decides to give great names to her children. She had shifted her attention to God. When Leah was not even expecting to give birth to children again, she conceived, and she named the boy ISSACHAR meaning 'God hath given me my hire.' So it is now all about God, not Jacob or Rachel. Even if Jacob refused to acknowledge the vital contributions of Leah, God had paid her dowry by satisfying her desires.

When it looked as if Leah had reached menopause, God decided to show His faithfulness. Leah became pregnant again, and the sixth boy was named ZEBULUN meaning good dowry "honour," If Racheal will not honour her, God had honoured her. What a great lesson for us all. Her attitude changed despite the fact that her situation seemed to remain unchanged.

> *"17And God hearkened unto Leah, and she conceived, and bare Jacob the fifth son. 18And Leah said, God hath given me my hire, because I have given my maiden to my husband: and she called his name Issachar. 19And Leah conceived again, and bare Jacob the sixth son. 20And Leah said, God hath endued me with a good dowry; now will my husband dwell with me, because I have born him six sons: and she called his name Zebulun. 21And afterwards she bare a daughter, and called her name Dinah"* (Genesis 30:17-21).

Unexpectedly, she became pregnant for the seventh time, but it was not a boy but the very first girl in the family. What a chance to put on her boxing gloves and give her name that will speak volume of her challenges, but she rather chose a very wonderful name DINAH meaning 'vindicated' 'Justified.' God had vindicated her what a consolation, no longer bitterness and anger but a complete surrender to the sovereignty and faithfulness of God.

> *"22And God remembered Rachel, and God hearkened to her and opened her womb. 23And she conceived, and bare a son; and said, God hath taken away my reproach: 24And she called*

*his name Joseph; and said, The Lord shall add
to me another son" (Genesis 30:22-24).*

When Rachel was finally pregnant, it looked as if
she had learnt her lessons. God could not have given
her Joseph before this time because the likelihood of
her using him as a bargaining asset was very high.
She named him JOSEPH meaning 'God had taken
away my humiliation.' This was very prophetic as
when she was naming Dan and Naphtali she was just
pretending to have joy. It was not strange then for
God to eventually use Joseph to erase the humiliation
of famine, division, unforgiveness, and shame in the
lineage of Jacob. Can you imagine if she had messed
up Joseph's life by giving him a wrong name that
may not have any bearing on his future? God had to
wait until Racheal had learnt her lesson.

In 1 Samuel 1, Hannah's prayer was not answered
until she realised that God is always purpose driven.
God needed a prophet, Hannah needed a son. She
did not desire a son so as to show off to her rival and
her children. Testimonies are not meant to be abused
but to showcase the divine plans and purposes of
God.

> *"17And it came to pass, when she was in hard
> labour, that the midwife said unto her, 'Fear
> not; thou shalt have this son also.' 18And it
> came to pass, as her soul was in departing, (for
> she died) that she called his name Benoni: but*

his father called him Benjamin" (Genesis 35:17-18).

We were informed of the conception of the second biological son of Rachel, but unfortunately, she went through so much pain and anguish during labour. This may be as a result of old age or other complications, but before she gave up the ghost, she managed to muster the name of the latest arrival. She was so overwhelmed with the situation and the circumstances surrounding the birth of this boy and therefore decided to name him BENONI meaning 'my suffering son.'

It is significant to note that in all the naming of the other children, it was whatever their mothers named them that they were called. Jacob was never involved or mentioned. However, on this particular occasion, the father had to step in maybe after learning by experience, the damage that names like are Ruben, Simeon, Levi and Naphtali had caused him and the whole family. To name this one as the son of suffering will not happen, so he quickly changed the name to BENJAMIN meaning 'son of the right hand.' What a destiny-changing name.

> *"And it came to pass, as her soul was in departing, (for she died) that she called his name Benoni: but his father called him Benjamin" (Genesis 35:18).*

Jacob had finally matured. Woken from his slumber, he had finally understood destiny. "Whatever you look at consistently is what you finally become," as claimed by one of my friends.

I can just picture Jacob shouting with every strength in him against the name Benoni. Because he was born in pain does not mean that he was to be forever associated with grief, but he would be a child of the right hand.

I choose to repeat myself that happiness is a choice, joy is a choice, and it takes personal decision to achieve this.

You are right on your way to your complete restoration because even the birds will and they must pay.

I am awaiting your testimony.

www.ingramcontent.com/pod-product-compliance
Lightning Source LLC
Chambersburg PA
CBHW071610040426
42452CB00008B/1299